Just Right Words

SLAM Poetry

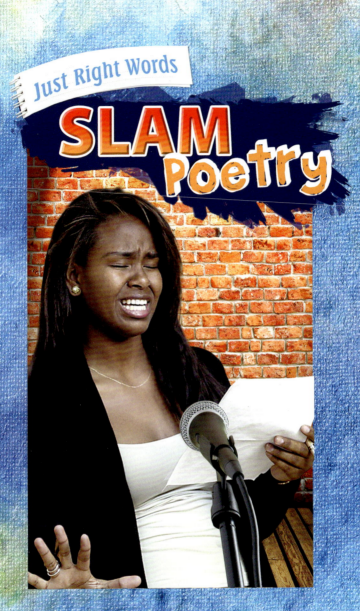

Elizabeth Siris Winchester

Consultants

Kenn Nesbitt
Children's Poet Laureate 2013–15

Publishing Credits

Rachelle Cracchiolo, M.S.Ed., *Publisher*
Conni Medina, M.A.Ed., *Managing Editor*
Nika Fabienke, Ed.D., *Series Developer*
June Kikuchi, *Content Director*
John Leach, *Assistant Editor*
Lee Aucoin, *Senior Graphic Designer*

TIME For Kids and the TIME For Kids logo are registered trademarks of TIME Inc. Used under license.

Image Credits: Cover and p.1 Michael Loccisano/Getty Images for Mad Over You; Reader's Guide page Derek Davis/Portland Press Herald via Getty Images; pp.4, 5 Bennett Raglin/Getty Images for DreamYard Project; p.6 dpa picture alliance/Alamy Stock Photo; p.7 Christian K. Lee/The Washington Post via Getty Images; p.8 Patrick Farrell/Miami Herald/MCT via Getty Images; p.9 Tim Mosenfelder/Getty Images; p.13 Philip Scalia/Alamy Stock Photo; p.14 ZUMA Press, Inc./Alamy Stock Photo; pp.14–15 Jonathan Newton/The Washington Post via Getty Images; p.16 Dimitrios Kambouris/Getty Images for Tony Awards Productions; pp.16–17 Yoon S. Byun/The Boston Globe via Getty Images; pp.18–19, 21 Bennett Raglin/Getty Images for DreamYard Project; p.23 Michael Loccisano/Getty Images for Mad Over You; p.27 Patrick Farrell/Miami Herald/MCT via Getty Images; p.31 Barry Chin/The Boston Globe via Getty Images; all other images from iStock and/or Shutterstock.

All companies and products mentioned in this book are registered trademarks of their respective owners or developers and are used in this book strictly for editorial purposes; no commercial claim to their use is made by the author or the publisher.

Library of Congress Cataloging-in-Publication Data

Names: Winchester, Elizabeth, author.
Title: Just right words : slam poetry / Elizabeth Siris Winchester.
Description: Huntington Beach, CA : Teacher Created Materials, 2017. | Includes index.
Identifiers: LCCN 2017017373 (print) | LCCN 2017033148 (ebook) | ISBN 9781425853556 (eBook) | ISBN 9781425849818 (pbk.)
Subjects: LCSH: Poetry slams--Juvenile literature. | Performance poetry--Juvenile literature. | Oral interpretation of poetry--Juvenile literature. | Poetry--Authorship--Juvenile literature.
Classification: LCC PN4151 (ebook) | LCC PN4151 .W55 2017 (print) | DDC 808.5/45--dc23
LC record available at https://lccn.loc.gov/2017017373

Teacher Created Materials

5301 Oceanus Drive
Huntington Beach, CA 92649-1030
http://www.tcmpub.com

ISBN 978-1-4258-4981-8

© 2018 Teacher Created Materials, Inc.
Printed in China WAI002

Table of Contents

It's a Poetry Slam!...4

Write On!..6

Word Warriors..12

You're a Poet, You Know It!............................18

Find Your Voice...26

Glossary 28

Index..29

Check It Out! 30

Try It!..31

About the Author 32

It's a Poetry Slam!

Slam poetry is a form of spoken word poetry. People write and perform it for others. But slam poets don't wear costumes or use **props** or music. Some poems have a **rhythmic** or musical sound when read aloud. Other poems don't.

Slam poets use words to express thoughts and make people feel something. Their words are powerful. Slam poetry is often about the author's identity, including his or her **race** or gender. Or it can be fun and silly.

There are rules for slam poetry competitions, known as *poetry slams*. But there are few rules for writing the actual poems. Slam poets write about anything. They use words as they wish and do not need to follow the usual grammar rules.

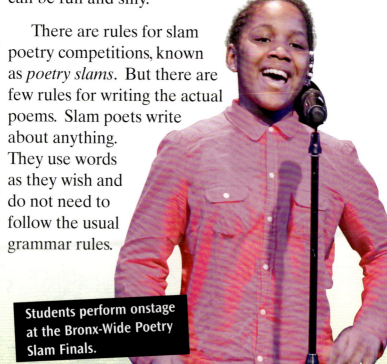

Students perform onstage at the Bronx-Wide Poetry Slam Finals.

About ME

Momma told me to know my story
She said, "Learn you and tell the world as you do"
To dream 3-point shots
but shoot to read everything
& give everything all you got
She warned about his stories found in schoolbooks given to me
Said be ready cause barely anyone in there will look like me
Think like me Like me
Then I found Poetry
Poetry like me
So I started writing
Started writing about me
About What I wanted to see
How I wanted to believe
In who I was to be
So I started writing to learn about me
ME

—½ Pint Poetics,
  Ravenswood
  Elementary School
  fifth graders,
  Chicago, Illinois

Write On!

People have always told stories. Poetry is one way to do so. A construction worker and poet named Marc Kelly Smith came up with a new way to share poetry with others. Smith started the poetry slam **movement**.

Smith felt that poets should be free to *not* follow rules. He thought poetry had lost its passion. In 1986, he started a weekly poetry reading. It was at a jazz club in Chicago, Illinois. His readings became popular. Smith hosted the first poetry slam at another Chicago jazz club. In poetry slams, judges from the audience score the poets. The scores are based on the writing and performance of the poetry.

Rhythmic Writers

Langston Hughes (LANG-stuhn HYOOZ) was an American poet. He wrote "jazz poetry." It had rhythms similar to the ones in blues and jazz music of the time.

Jordan Perry, 17, recites one of his poems in front of the Martin Luther King Jr. Memorial.

Slam poetry and poetry slams quickly spread across the United States. Slam poets shared their work in cafés and clubs. They read at open mic nights. These are events where inexperienced people perform for an audience. Anyone can go on stage to sing, tell jokes, perform poetry, and more. Slam poetry spread to other countries, too. Younger writers began to take part. In 1990, the first National Poetry Slam took place. It was held in San Francisco, California.

James Kass helped bring slam poetry to teens. He started the group Youth Speaks in 1996. Other groups teach slam poetry to elementary school kids.

That Rules!

Poetry slam rules can vary, but these are common:
- Poets compete as individuals or on teams.
- Poets must perform poems that they wrote themselves.
- Poets get three minutes to read one poem.
- Costumes, props, and instruments are not allowed.
- Judges are chosen from the audience. They give scores to the poets, which are used to figure out who competes in the next rounds and who wins.

James Kass (center) and Youth Speaks poets attend a premiere party for HBO's *Brave New Voices* and Youth Speaks in San Francisco, California.

TV Time

A television show that aired for five years also helped make slam poetry popular. It was called *Def Poetry Jam*. It allowed people to watch slam poets in action.

Earth Day

Trash on the ground ends up in the sea.
People use too much electricity.
Careless people leak oil into the sea
    like it was a dumpster.
All of this is starting to destroy her.
People pollute the air with their cars.
We don't want to end up like Mars.
People use way too much paper.
Global warming is making water into vapor.
Here's the problem: too much pollution.
Reduce, reuse, recycle is the solution.
We are like a **tsunami** washing away the earth.
Don't you think it hurts?
So these are some things we all can do
To stop making the earth feel blue.

1. Recycle more and throw out less trash.
2. Use less electricity by turning off the lights that are not in use.
3. Don't drive, instead bike or walk.
4. Use less paper cause it's wasting trees.

Make sure you do all of these.
Save the earth! Save the earth! Save the earth!
Don't be mean, be green!

—½ Pint Poetics, Lara Elementary
   Academy second graders,
   Chicago, Illinois

Poems with a Purpose

Read the poem aloud. Many people write and perform slam poetry to encourage change.

- What words or phrases do you find most powerful?
- How can you use your voice to best express them?
- How does this poem make you feel?
- What kind of change do these poets hope to bring about?
- Why do you think the authors wrote the poem?

Word Warriors

The Nuyorican (new-yo-REEK-in) Poets Cafe is in New York City. It opened in 1973. A group of Puerto Rican writers started it. The café is known for its open mic nights and Friday night poetry slams. Top poets compete in the Friday slams. People wait in lines to listen to slam poets.

Top performers can join the café's National Poetry Slam team. Groups from all over the United States compete in this event. People can compete in a group or perform **solo**. The café has other programs for poets, musicians, and actors of all ages.

Get to Work

The Nuyorican sometimes holds poetry slam **workshops** for kids. The workshops start with a performance by poets. Then, the students are placed in small groups so they can write about their own experiences.

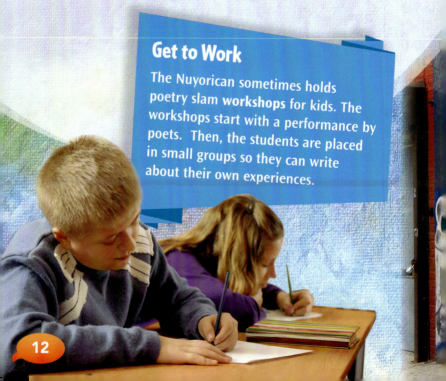

Poetry of the People

"Slam poetry events involve a lot of **interaction**," Daniel Gallant explains. He is the Nuyorican's executive director. "Slam poets rely on energy from the audience."

Poets in Chicago

Kuumba Lynx (KOOM-buh LIHNKS) is an urban arts youth group in Chicago. It was founded by Jaquanda Villegas (juh-KWAN-duh vee-YEY-guhs) and Jacinda Bullie (hah-SIHN-duh BUL-ee) more than 20 years ago. The group provides a safe place where teens can express their thoughts. In the group, teens connect with poetry through the use of hip-hop. Villegas says, "Like the **MC** in hip-hop, the slam poet has the power to move the crowd!"

STOP! THINK...

This photo shows a teen performing for an audience at a poetry slam.

- What emotions do you think the poet is feeling?
- What clues in the photo give you an idea of how the poet might feel?
- What do you think the poem could be about?

In 2008, the group started a program for kids ages 8 to 14. It is called ½ Pint Poetics. Kids are taught to think and write about "class, race, gender, and global impact," says Bullie. School teams take part in a poetry slam each year. The slam ends with a hip-hop concert.

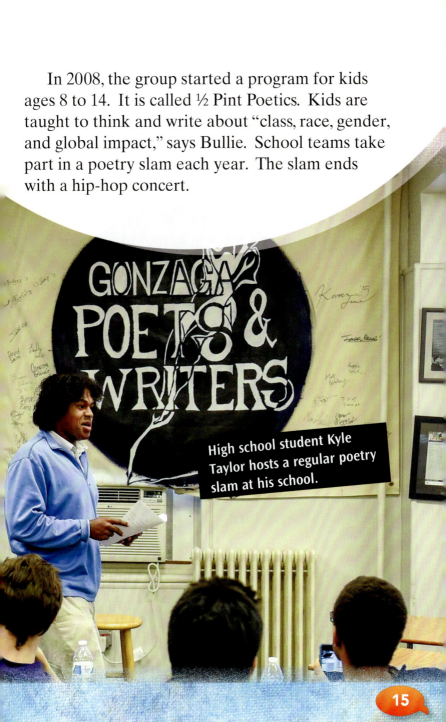

High school student Kyle Taylor hosts a regular poetry slam at his school.

Poets in San Francisco

Youth Speaks is based in San Francisco. It is for people ages 13 to 24. The group has programs across the country and around the world. It created the first national youth poetry slam in 1997. This event is called Brave New Voices. It takes place in a different U.S. city every year.

"We think every young person has a voice, and we want to work with youth to find their voice and present it," says Kass. "I started Youth Speaks to give young people a space to define who they are."

He Diggs It!

The hip-hop musical *Hamilton* is a Broadway smash hit. Daveed (dah-VEED) Diggs won a Tony Award® for playing the roles of Thomas Jefferson and the Marquis de Lafayette (mahr-KEE duh lah-fah-YEHT). He took part in Youth Speaks when he was in high school. He says poetry slams are the reason for his success.

Teens Talk
"I knew how much writing meant to me when I was young," Kass says. He suggests that kids watch slam poetry videos and see it live. "The most important thing is to be yourself and have fun."

You're a Poet, You Know It!

"Spoken word poetry is the art of performance poetry. It involves creating poetry that doesn't just want to sit on paper. Something about it demands it be heard out loud," says Sarah Kay.

Kay was in a poetry group in college with another student named Phil Kaye. Together, they started Project VOICE. The group teaches kids in all grades about spoken word poetry. The group has worked with hundreds of schools in over 20 countries.

Sarah writes poems to figure things out. Phil likes writing and sharing poems with others. Think about the words and meanings of this poem as you read it. Say it aloud, with feeling.

DreamYard Project hosted the Bronx-Wide Poetry Slam in 2016.

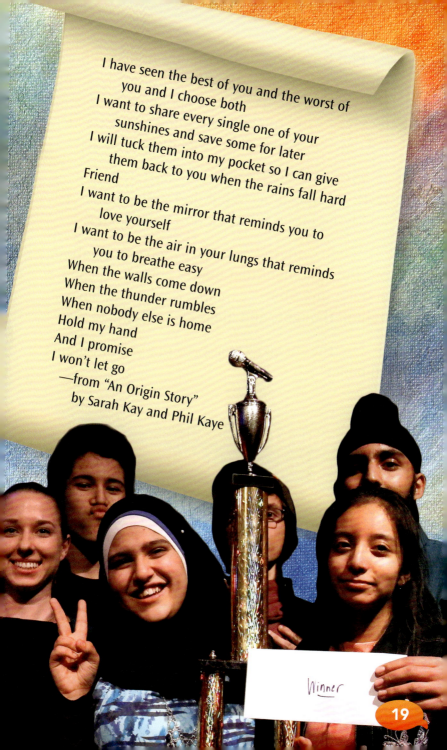

I have seen the best of you and the worst of you and I choose both
I want to share every single one of your sunshines and save some for later
I will tuck them into my pocket so I can give them back to you when the rains fall hard
Friend
I want to be the mirror that reminds you to love yourself
I want to be the air in your lungs that reminds you to breathe easy
When the walls come down
When the thunder rumbles
When nobody else is home
Hold my hand
And I promise
I won't let go
—from "An Origin Story" by Sarah Kay and Phil Kaye

Phil Kaye found slam poetry in high school. "I thought poetry was something I didn't like until I saw someone…perform a spoken word poem," he says. "I still remember feeling, 'Wow! I can't believe this is something I'm allowed to do.'"

Project VOICE helps kids start writing with three big questions: What do I write about? How do I write about it? How do I perform it?

"Poetry doesn't necessarily have to be about a big, huge moment that makes you cry. It can be about a tiny thing," explains Kaye. "We have a million thoughts and ideas every day."

Use these two exercises to put your thoughts on paper!

Exercise 1: List It!

Make a list of three things you know to be true. The only rules are to use details and to not think too hard. For example, Kaye likes the Los Angeles Lakers, Friday afternoons, and chili. Kaye might say he likes chili because when he was little, his dad used to make it with him.

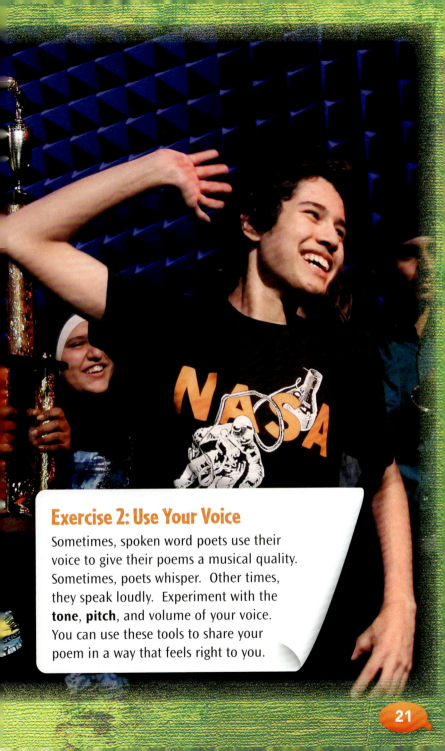

Exercise 2: Use Your Voice

Sometimes, spoken word poets use their voice to give their poems a musical quality. Sometimes, poets whisper. Other times, they speak loudly. Experiment with the **tone**, **pitch**, and volume of your voice. You can use these tools to share your poem in a way that feels right to you.

Poetry Rules!

There are three main categories of poetry. Lyric poems tell a person's thoughts or feelings. Narrative poetry tells a story. Dramatic poems use characters to act out a story. Each of these categories includes many forms of poems. Slam poetry is a form of lyric poetry.

When it comes to writing, slam poetry doesn't have any rules. But other types require poets to follow rules. For example, haiku has a certain number of syllables and lines. Other poems have rhyme patterns.

All poems are creative ways for people to express themselves. Rhythm is the way the language flows and sounds in a poem. Poetry often includes patterns known as *meter*.

Haiku

This Japanese poetry form has 17 syllables that are broken up into three lines. The first and third lines have five syllables. The second line has seven syllables. The poem often includes a word that tells or hints at the season the poet is writing about.

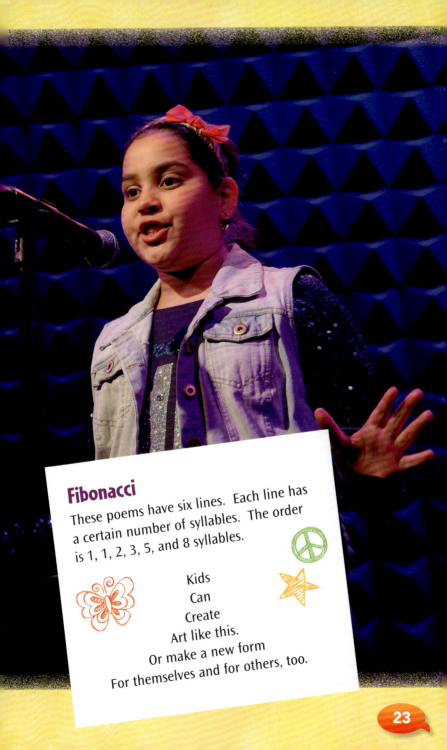

Fibonacci

These poems have six lines. Each line has a certain number of syllables. The order is 1, 1, 2, 3, 5, and 8 syllables.

Kids
Can
Create
Art like this.
Or make a new form
For themselves and for others, too.

How to Throw a Poetry Slam

½ Pint Poetics offers these tips for getting started:

🔊 Gather a crew of teachers, artists, students, and community members.

🔊 Get kids interested by having a slam poetry performance at a school assembly. Afterward, have students sign up to take part in a poetry slam.

🔊 Decide whether you will have a slam team or individual poets.

🔊 Classes could compete against each other, or school against school. Or kids could perform as individuals.

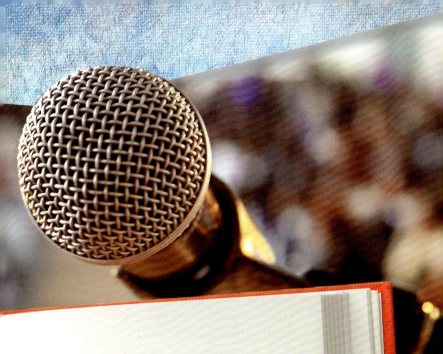

🔊 Structure the slam in a way that lessens competition. Celebrate strengths.

🔊 Figure out details. Who will compete? When and where will the slam take place? How will you invite the community?

🔊 Record the event. Find someone to take pictures and make a video.

🔊 Make it fun with food, giveaways, judges, hosts, a DJ (to play music between poems), and a full audience. Make sure participants know the rules of the poetry slam. The goal is for everyone to exchange ideas and have fun!

Find Your Voice

> The sun rises. It's time to get out of bed.
> Your mom rushing you along
>   is something you dread.
> Instead of getting angry, think about
>   all there is to see and do
> What exciting things might happen to you?
> Write them down, you never know just
>   where your thoughts might let you go!

Why not give slam poetry a try? Use the information throughout this book to help you get started. Remember that there are no rules for writing slam poetry. Find your voice and be real. "A writer is someone who thinks and has ideas about the world," says Jacinda Bullie of Kuumba Lynx. "We're all writers. Some just haven't put their thoughts on paper yet.

A Winning Writer

In 2012, Santino Panzica won the TFK Poetry Contest. Santino was only 12 when he won! The next year, he published his first book of poems. It is called *The Man-Eating Lemon*.

Contest Time

TIME For Kids holds an annual poetry contest. It is open to kids ages 8 to 13 in the United States. Kids can write and send in poems that are funny and rhyme. They must be original and not copy another poet's work.

Glossary

interaction—when people communicate or react to each other

MC—short for *master of ceremonies*; the person in charge of the microphone

movement—a series of acts working toward an end

pitch—a quality of sound that can be high or low

props—objects used by performers to create a certain effect

race—belonging to a group of people with the same ancestry

rhythmic—having a pattern of sounds or movements

solo—alone

tone—quality of spoken sound

tsunami—a large sea wave caused by an earthquake, volcano, or other changes underwater

workshops—educational meetings or discussions that allow people to learn about or explore a specific topic

Index

½ Pint Poetics, 5, 10, 14, 24

Brave New Voices, 9, 16

Bronx-Wide Poetry Slam, 4, 18

Bullie, Jacinda, 14, 26

Def Poetry Jam, 9

Diggs, Daveed, 16

Fibonacci, 23

Gallant, Daniel, 13

haiku, 22

Hamilton, 16

Hughes, Langston, 6

Kass, James, 8–9, 16–17

Kay, Sarah, 18–19

Kaye, Phil, 18–20

Kuumba Lynx, 14, 26

National Poetry Slam, 8, 12

Nuyorican Poets Cafe, 12–13

open mic night, 8, 12

Perry, Jordan, 7

Project VOICE, 18, 20

Smith, Marc Kelly, 6

Taylor, Kyle, 15

Villegas, Jaquanda, 14

Youth Speaks, 8–9, 16

Check It Out!

Books

Regan, Dian Curtis. 2010. *Barnyard Slam*. Holiday House.

Swados, Elizabeth. 2002. *Hey You! C'mere! A Poetry Slam*. Arthur A. Levine Books.

Videos

LPS Media. *Wetherbee 3rd and 4th Grade Poetry Slam*.

Mali, Taylor. *On Girls Lending Pens*.

MentorTEAM. *Mentor Grade 6 Poetry Slam!*

Project VOICE. *An Origin Story*.

TED-Ed. *Miss Gayle's 5 Steps to Slam Poetry*.

THNKR. *Kioni "Popcorn" Marshall: Prodigy Poet*.

Websites

½ Pint Poetics. www.kuumbalynx.com/half-pint-poetics-2/.

Nuyorican Poets Cafe. www.nuyorican.org.

Project VOICE. www.projectvoice.co.

Youth Speaks. www.youthspeaks.org.

Try It!

Perform your poetry! Imagine that your school is hosting a poetry slam and needs kids to take part. You accept the challenge.

- 🔊 What will you write about?
- 🔊 Will your poem focus on a small moment or a big idea?
- 🔊 Use some of the tips in this book to get started. Share your poem with a friend.
- 🔊 Practice performing. Slam poets play with their voice to get their message across. You could whisper, yell, or even break into song.

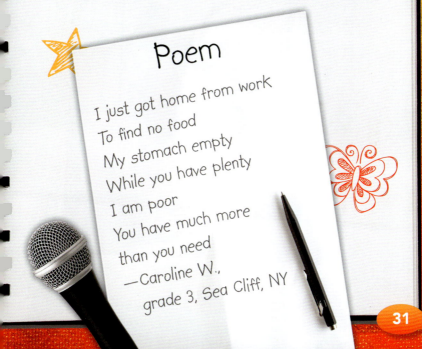

Poem

I just got home from work
To find no food
My stomach empty
While you have plenty
I am poor
You have much more
than you need
—Caroline W.,
grade 3, Sea Cliff, NY

About the Author

Elizabeth Siris Winchester has written for *TIME FOR KIDS* for almost 20 years. She has covered a range of topics from bullying, bats, and butterflies to amazing kids and groundbreaking figures. She is grateful to have found work that she enjoys and finds meaningful. She thanks her three kids for inspiring her often. She also loves running, yoga, baking, music, dogs, and especially time with friends and family.